INSIDE THE MIND OF A.I

KEYWORDS, PUZZLES, LINE ART AND SMOKE

CREATED BY
DANIEL MORENO

A BEST SELLING INTERACTIVE ART SERIES

Word From the Author

Thank you to all who supported me on my journey into the realm of creating books. I hope that this content inspires you to visit A.I art generating software and give it a try for yourselves. The combinations that can be created are genuinely astonishing. In the following pages, you will see some of the artwork that I generated using certain keywords, the likelihood of recreating an exact image is mathematically improbable so even using the same word combination will generate a whole new image. Enjoy!

TALK TO US
Any questions please email us @
Deejaysbookstore@gmail.com

TABLE OF CONTENTS || A.I GENERATED ART

Page # / Type of Art

1) Book Cover
2) Words From the Author
3) Table Of Contents
4) Maze
5) Maze
6) Maze
7) Smoke
8) Smoke
9) Smoke
10) Line
11) Line
12) Maze
13) Maze
14) Maze
15) Smoke
16) Smoke
17) Smoke
18) Maze
19) Maze
20) Maze
21) Maze
22) Maze
23) Smoke
24) Smoke
25) Smoke
26) Smoke
27) Smoke
28) Line
29) End

A.I GENERATION
#1

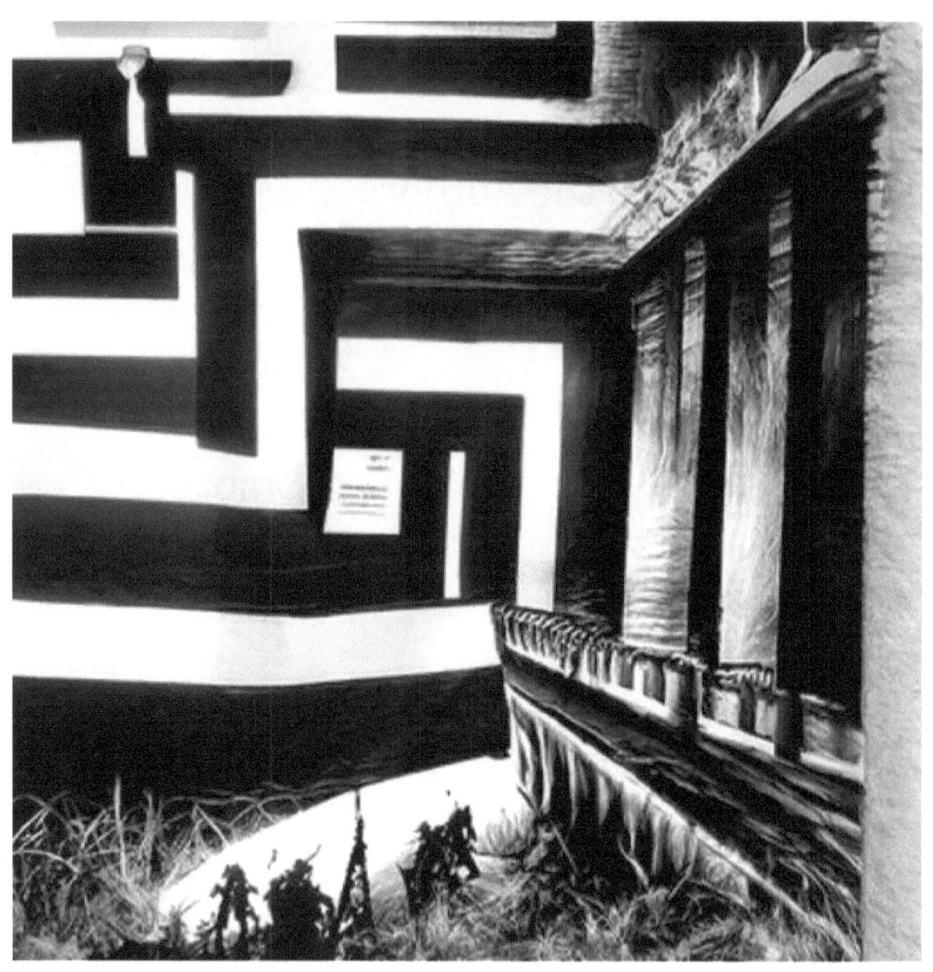

thin dark line art, intricate death maze, black and white, complex, interesting, realistic

A.I GENERATION #2

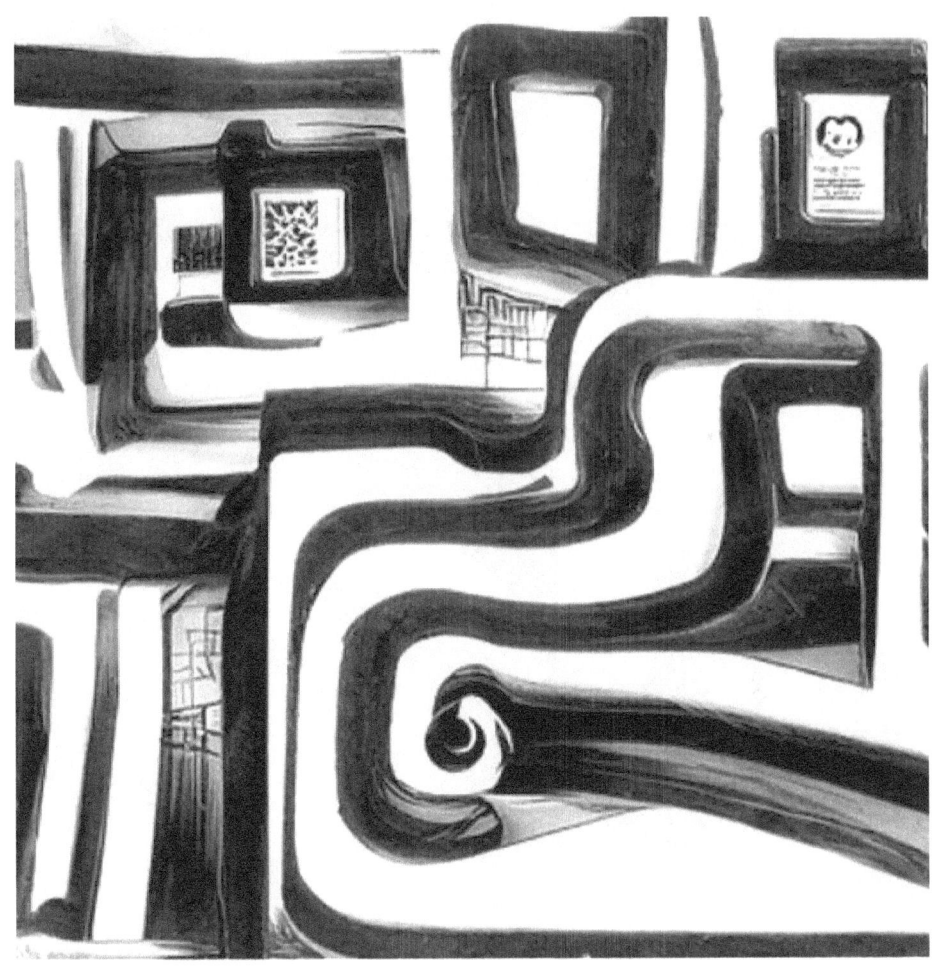

line art, intricate boxed swirly maze, black and white, complex, interesting, futuristic

A.I GENERATION #3

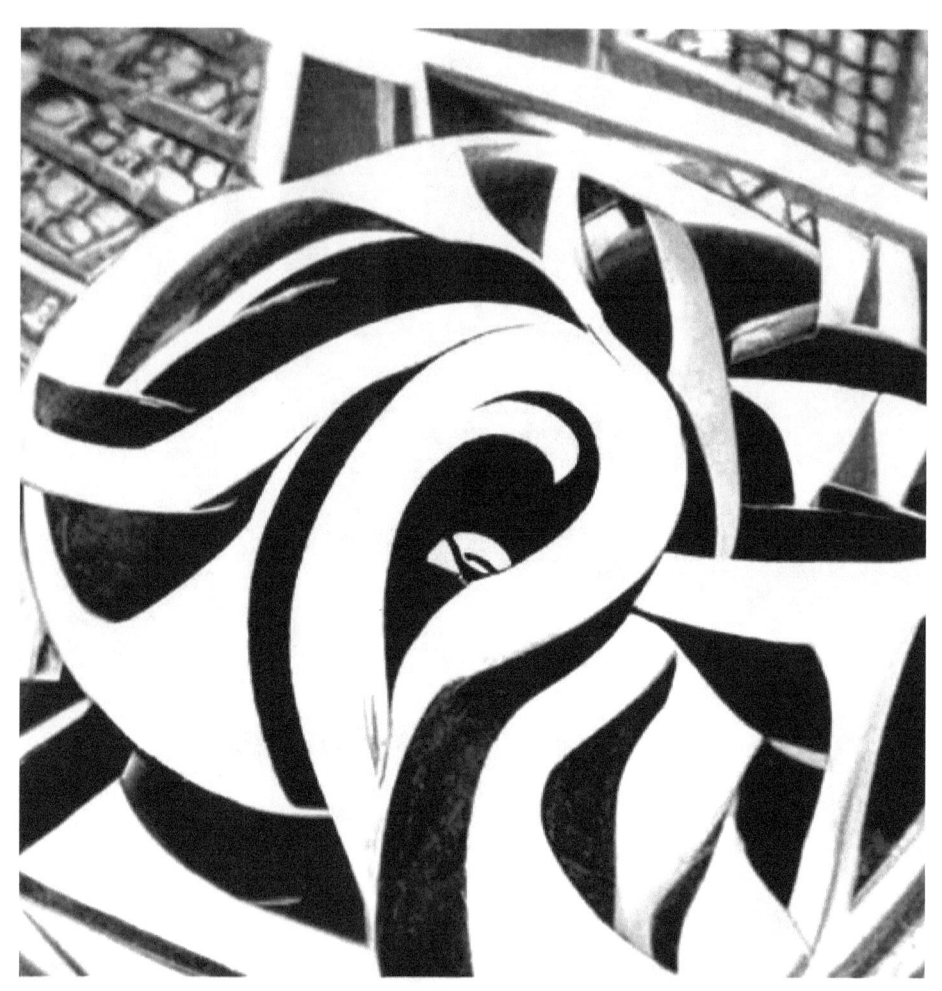

sharp, shaded, line art, intricate circle swirly maze, black and white, complex, interesting, futuristic

A.I GENERATION
#4

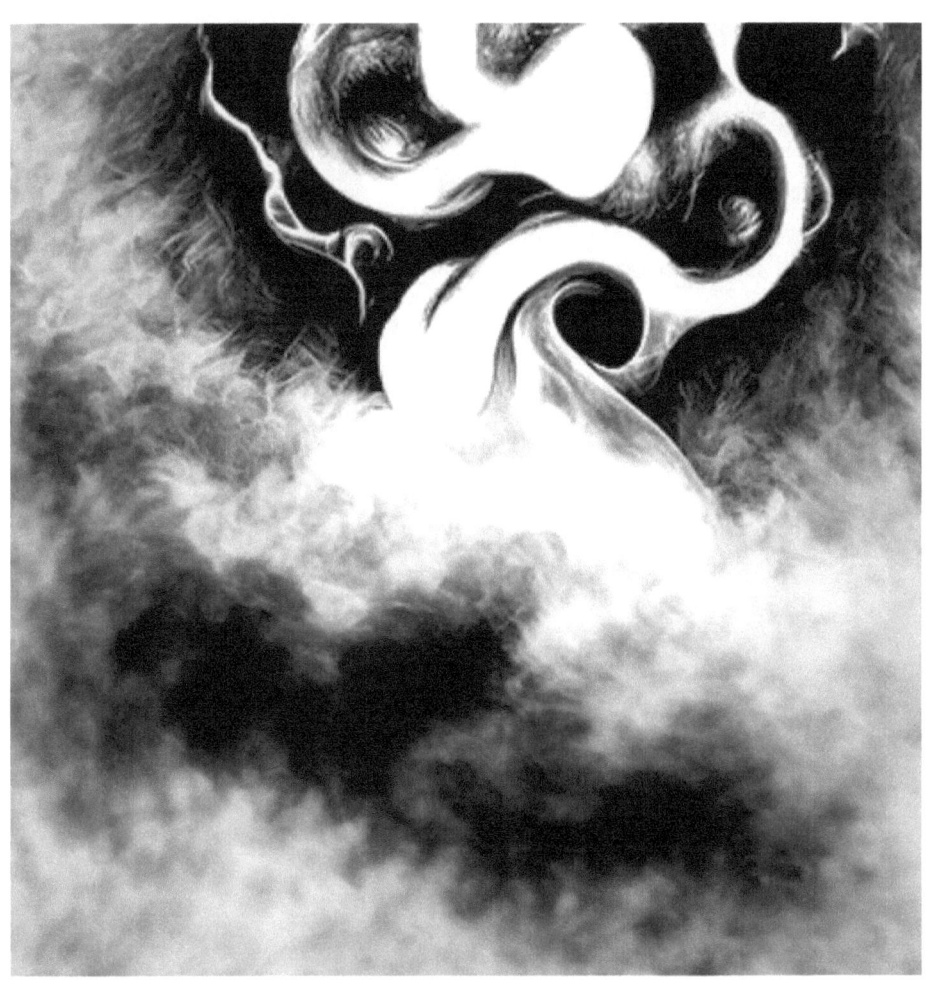

smokey clouds, dark line art, intricate death maze, keyhole, black and white, complex, interesting, realistic

A.I GENERATION
#5

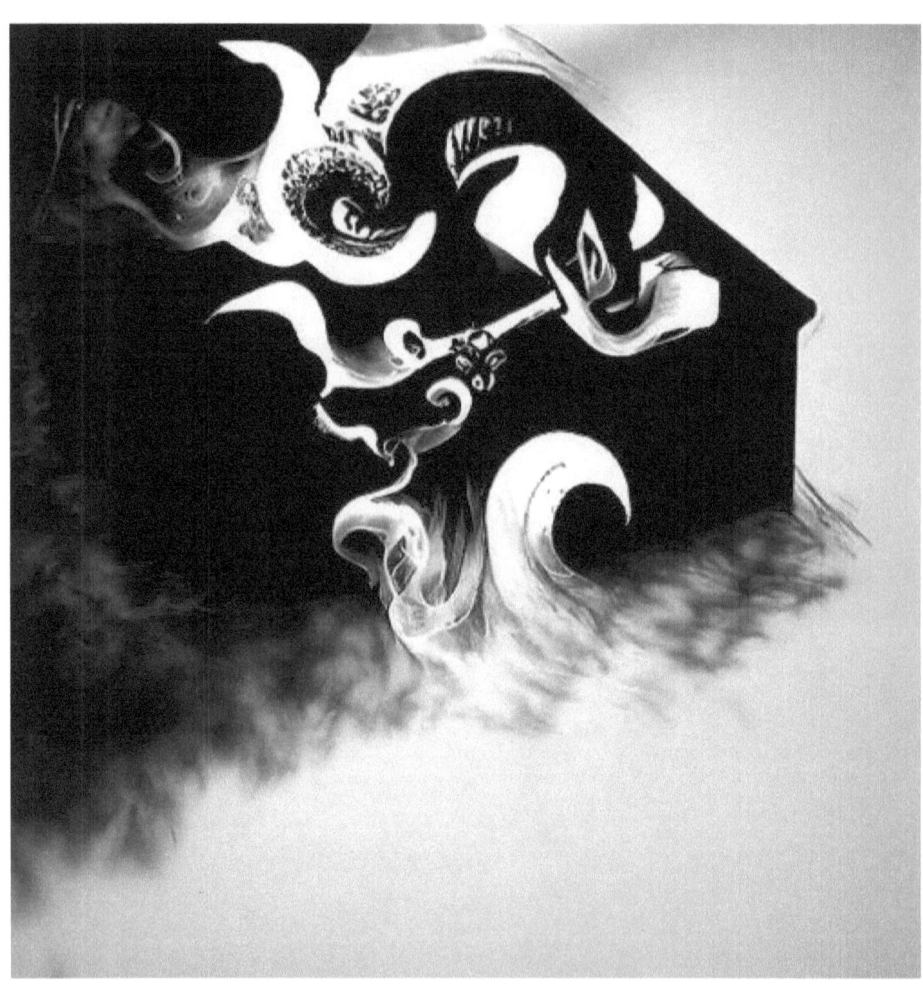

smoke clouds, dark line art, intricate death maze, keyhole, black and white, complex, interesting, realistic

A.I GENERATION #6

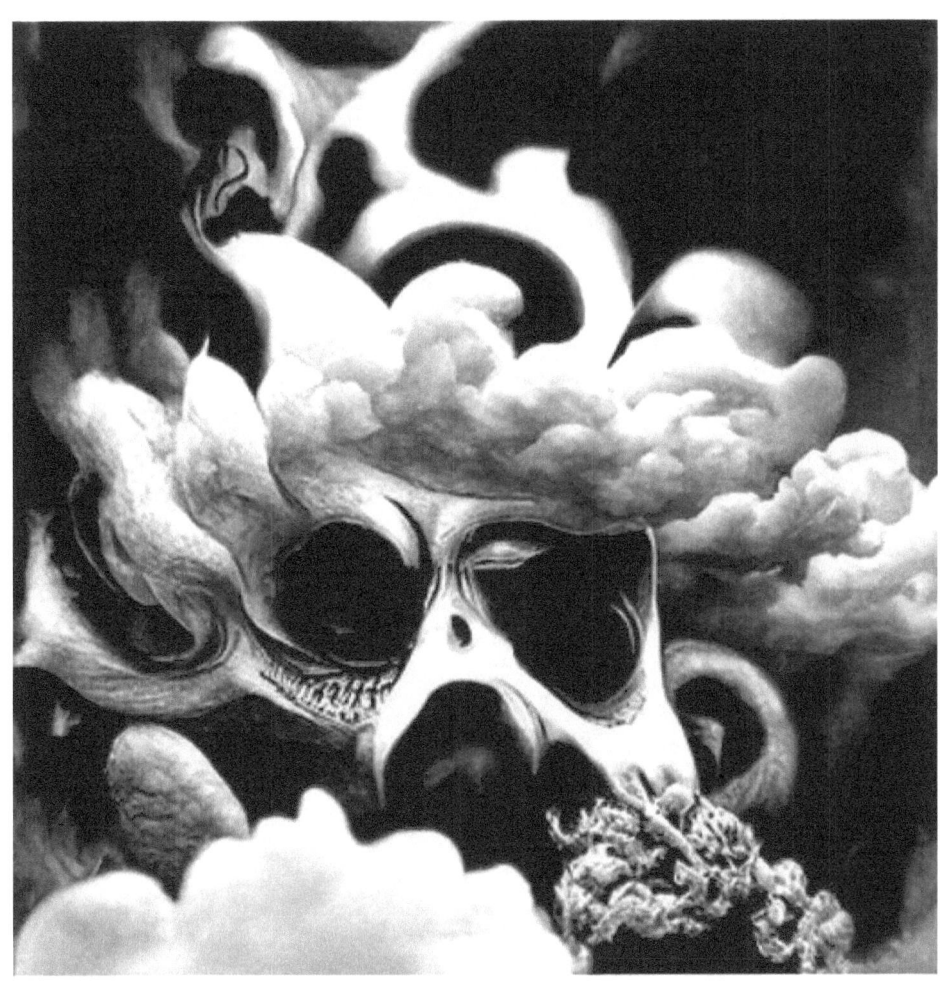

clustered smokey clouds, dark line art, intricate death maze, skull, black and white, complex, interesting, realistic

A.I GENERATION
#7

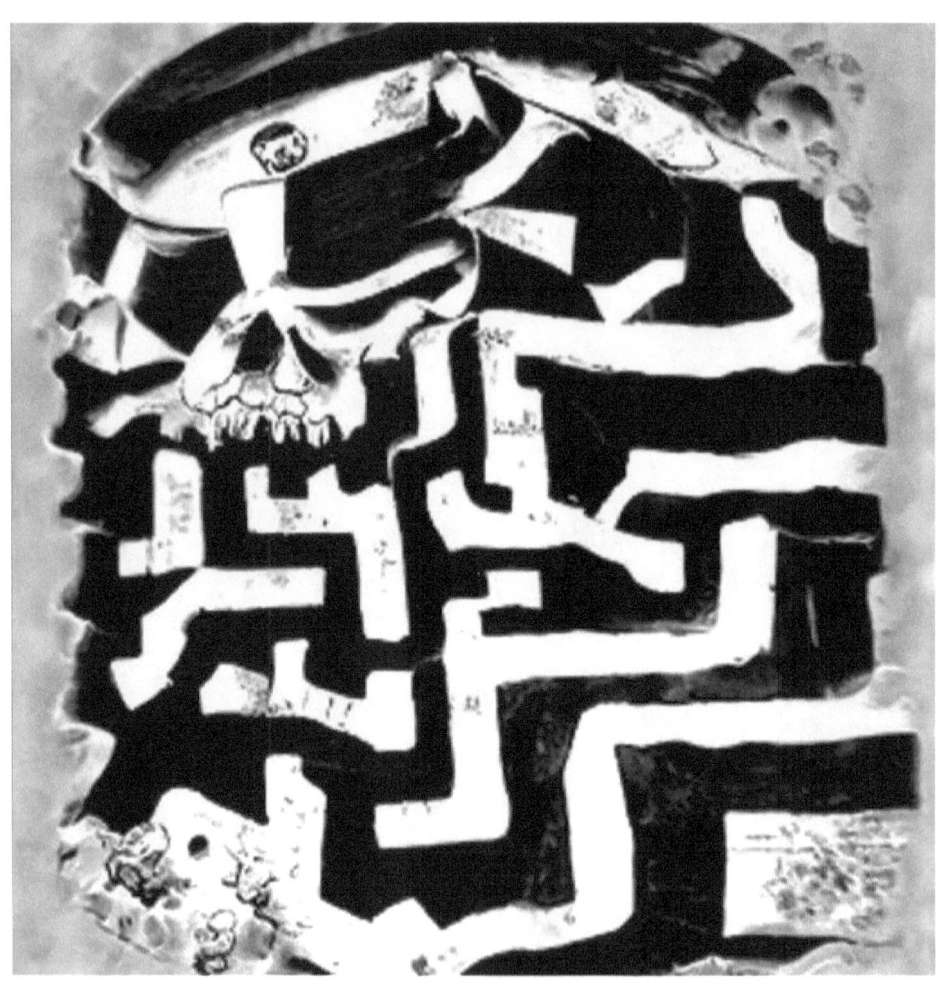

war, thin dark line art, intricate maze with small skulls, black and white, complex, interesting, realistic

A.I GENERATION
#8

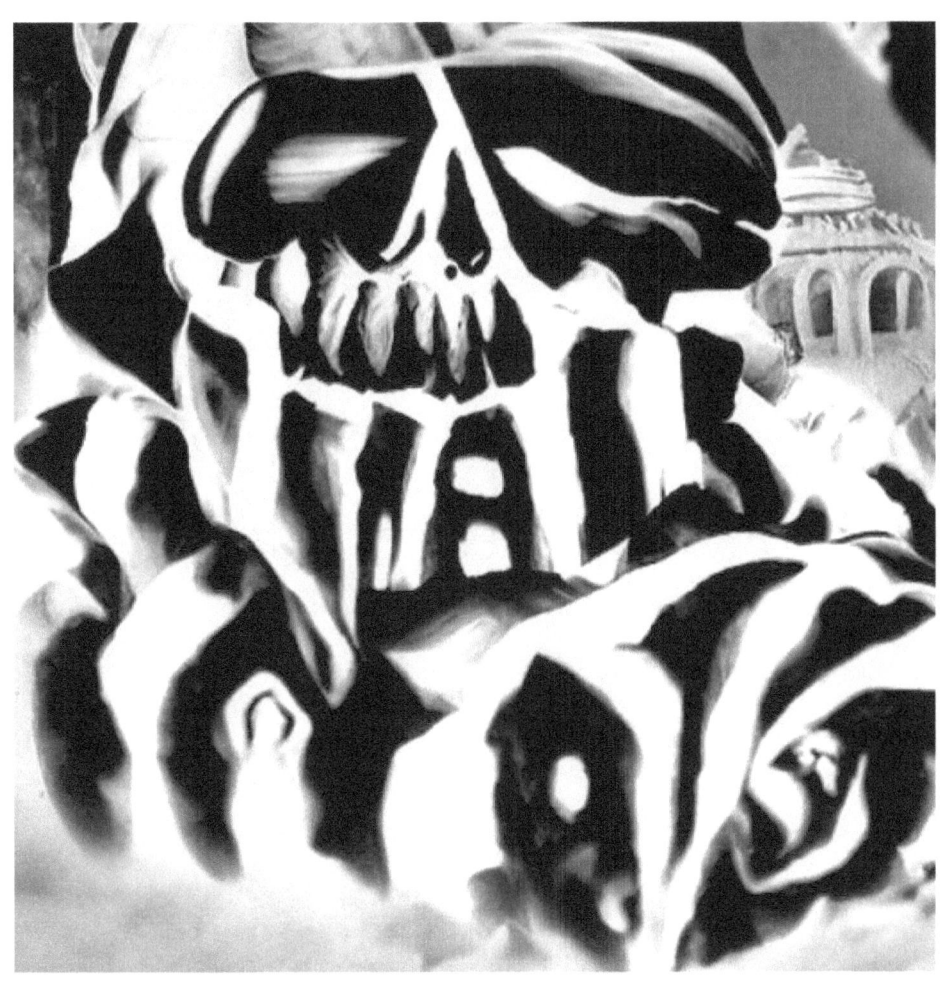

skulls, war banners, thin dark line art, intricate death maze, black and white, complex, interesting, realistic

A.I GENERATION
#9

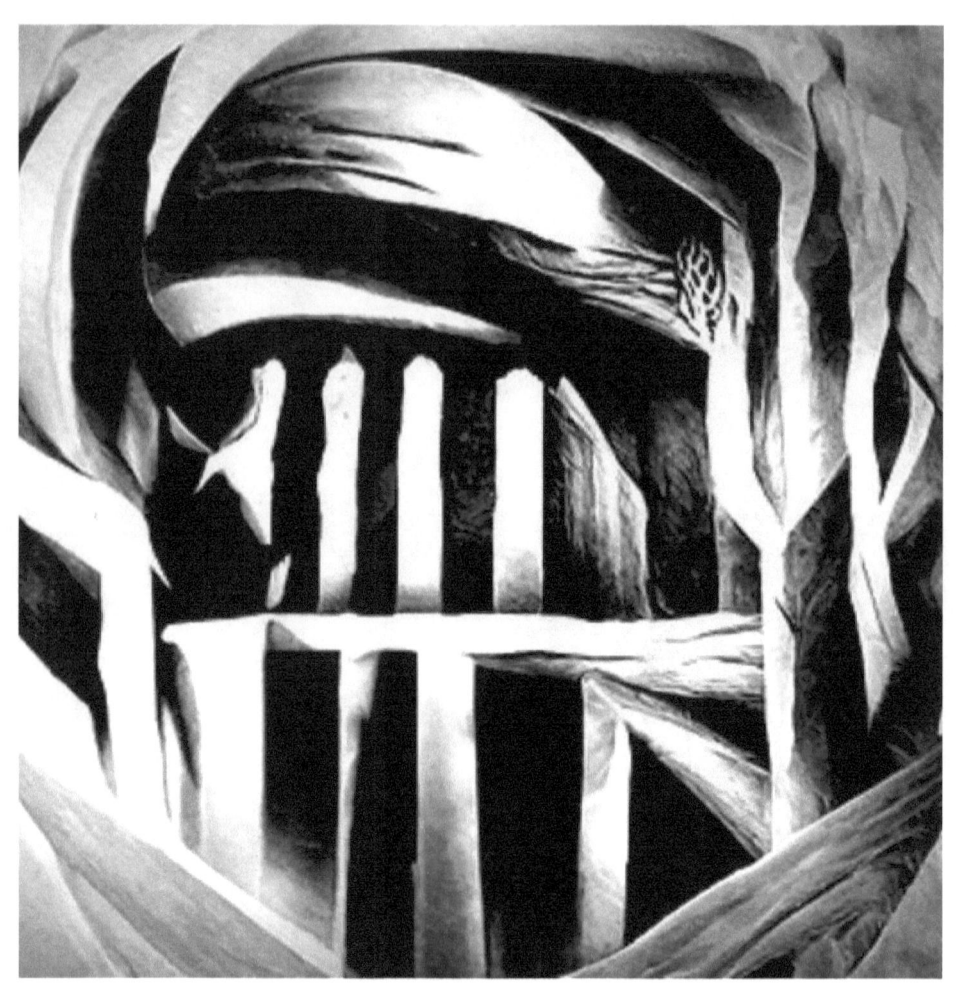

thin dark line art, intricate death maze, black and white, complex, interesting, realistic

A.I GENERATION
#10

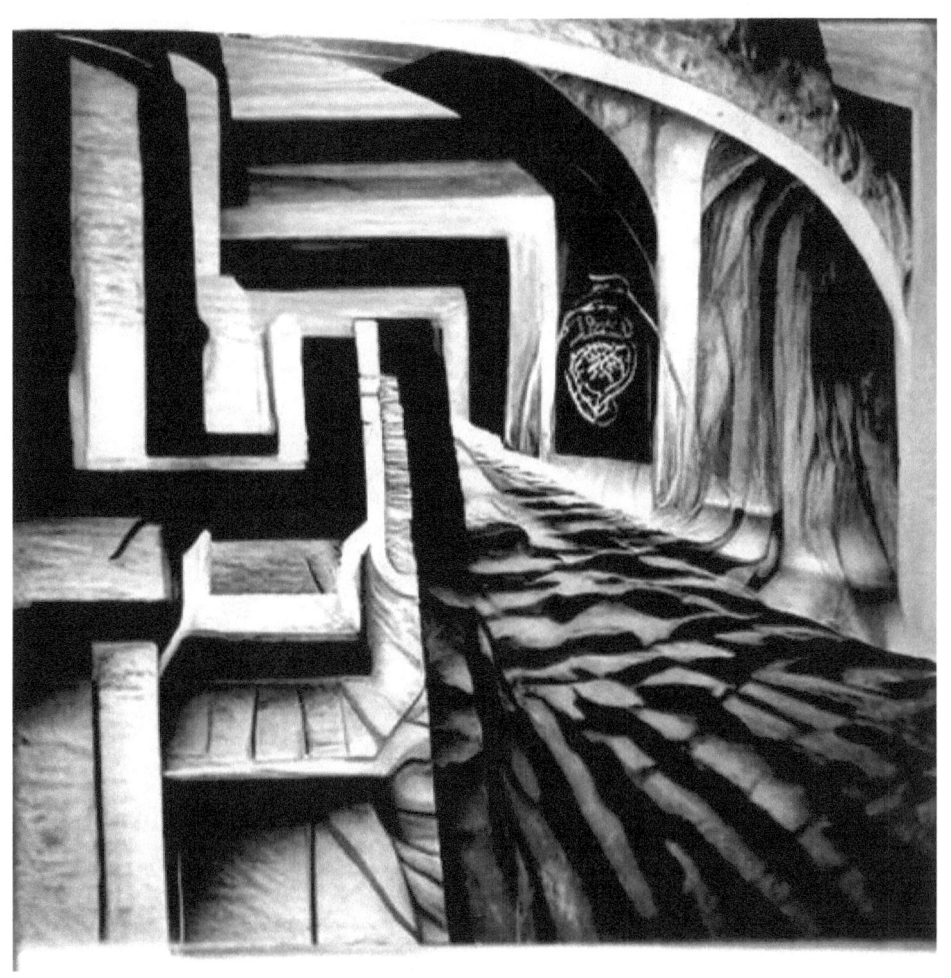

thin dark line art, intricate death maze, keyhole, black and white, complex, interesting, realistic

A.I GENERATION
#11

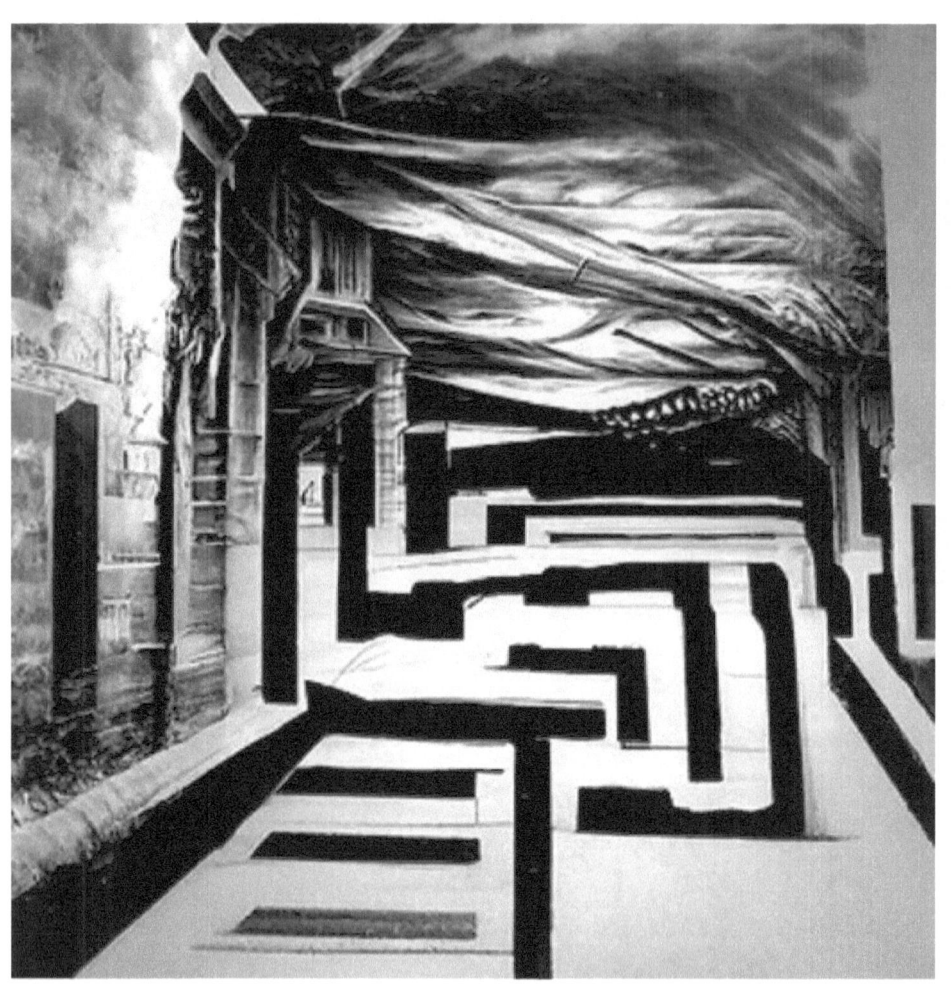

thin dark line art, intricate death maze, black and white, complex, interesting, realistic

A.I GENERATION
#12

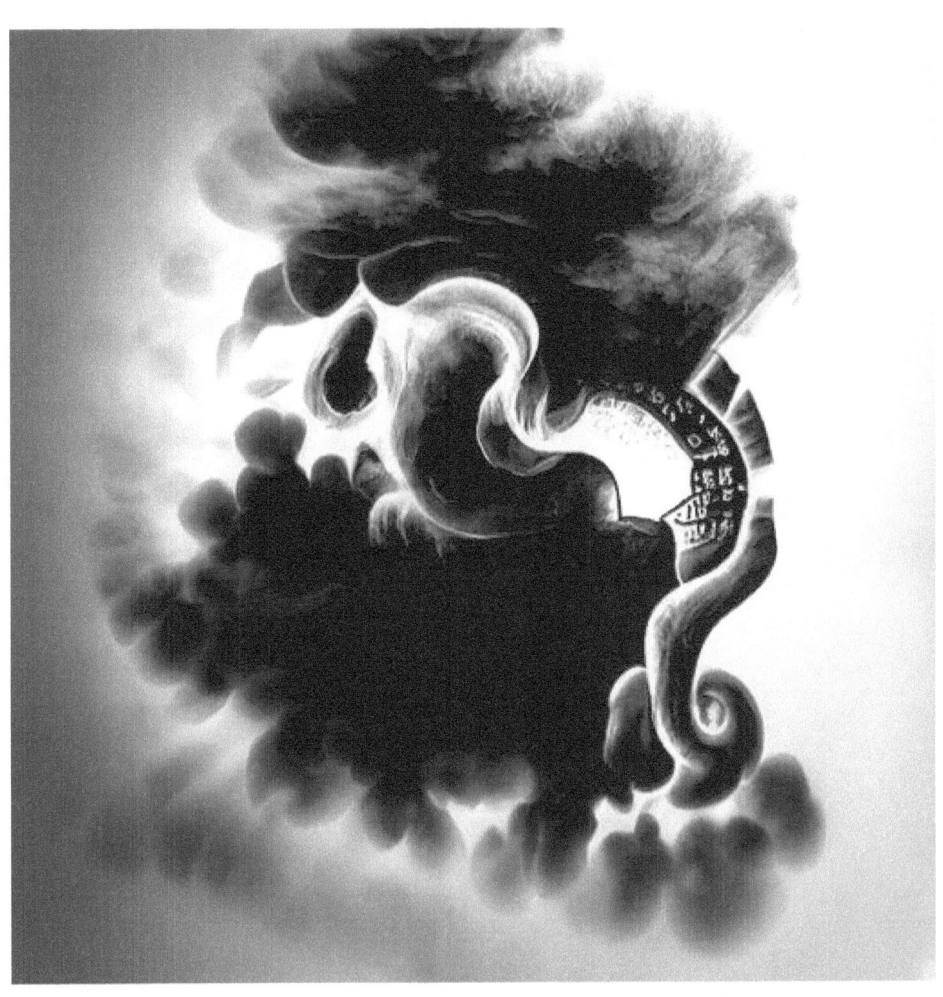

smokey clouds, dark line art, intricate death maze, keyhole, black and white, complex, interesting, realistic

A.I GENERATION
#13

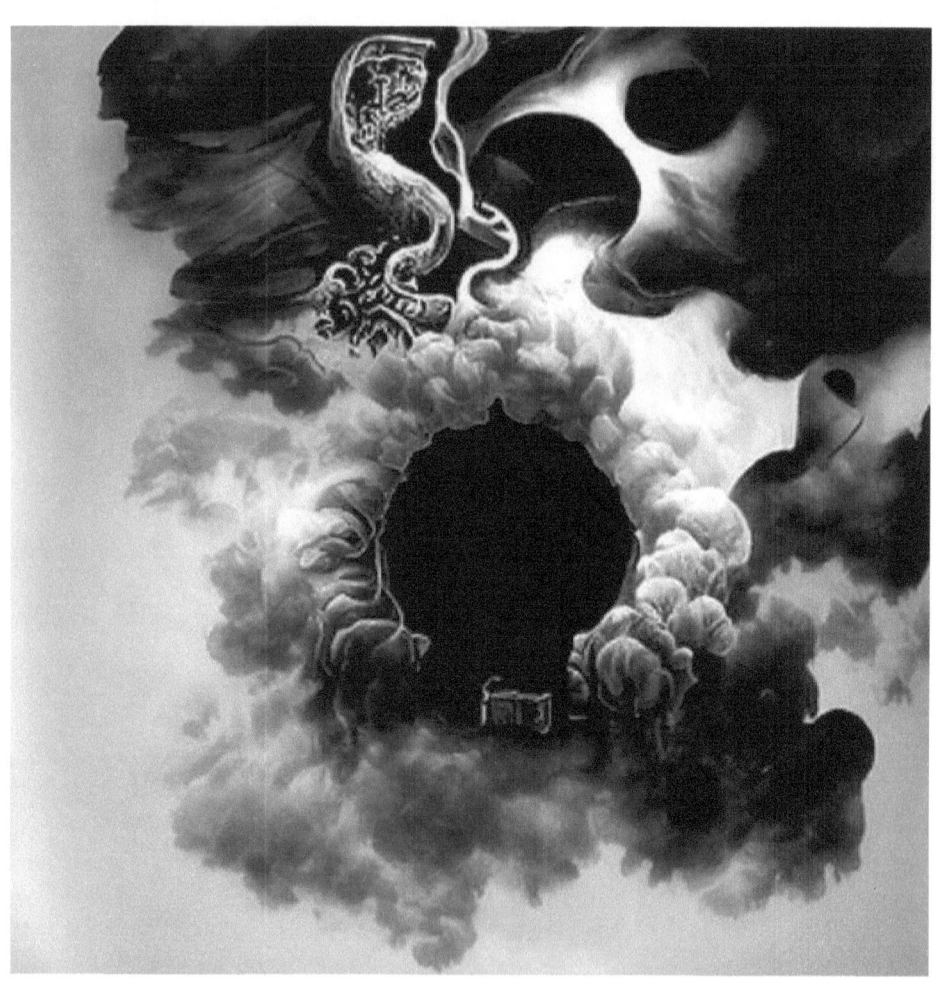

smokey clouds, dark line art, intricate death maze, keyhole, black and white, complex, interesting, realistic

A.I GENERATION #14

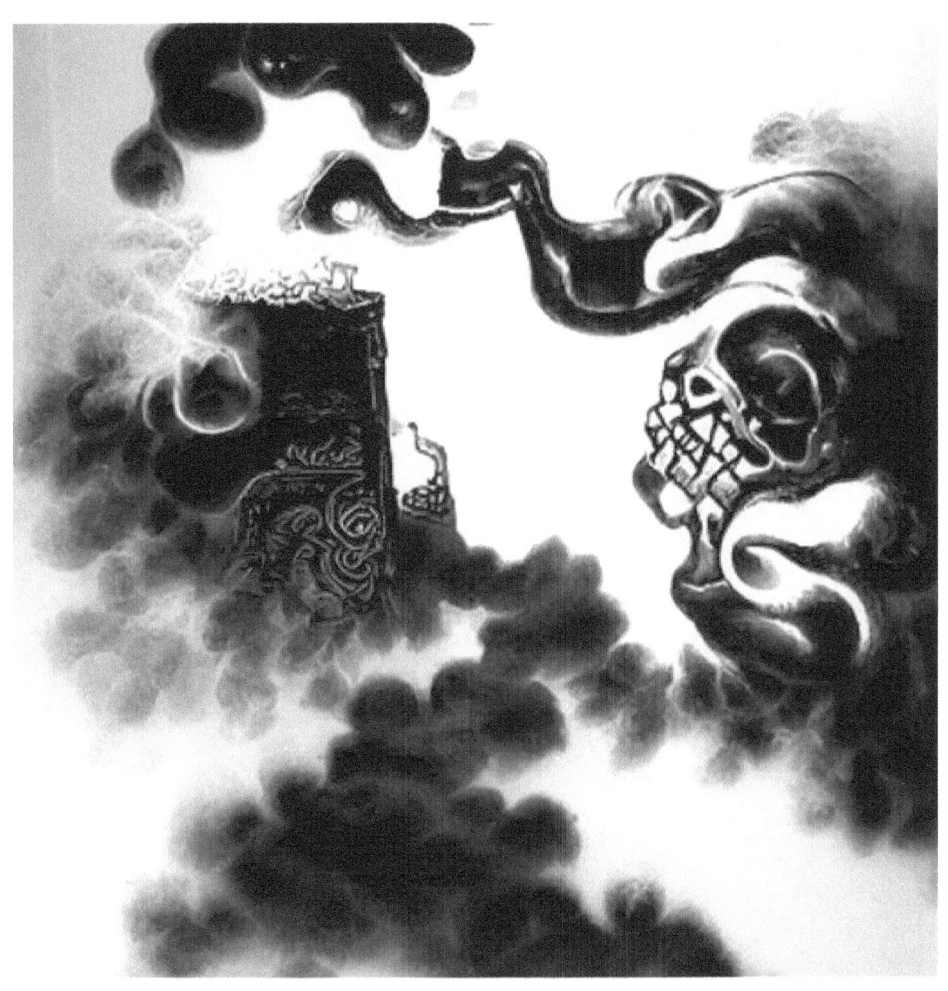

smokey clouds, dark line art, intricate death maze, keyhole, black and white, complex, interesting, realistic

A.I GENERATION
#15

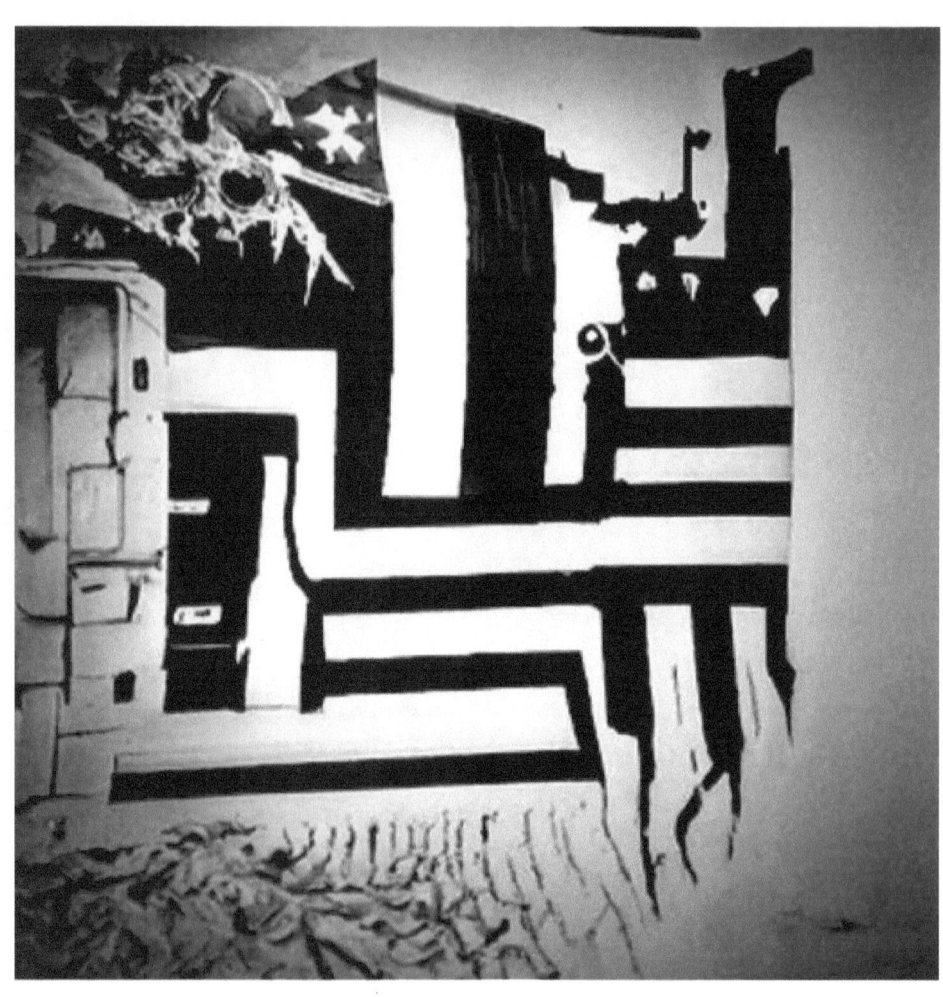

war time, thin dark line art, intricate death maze, black and white, complex, interesting, realistic

A.I GENERATION #16

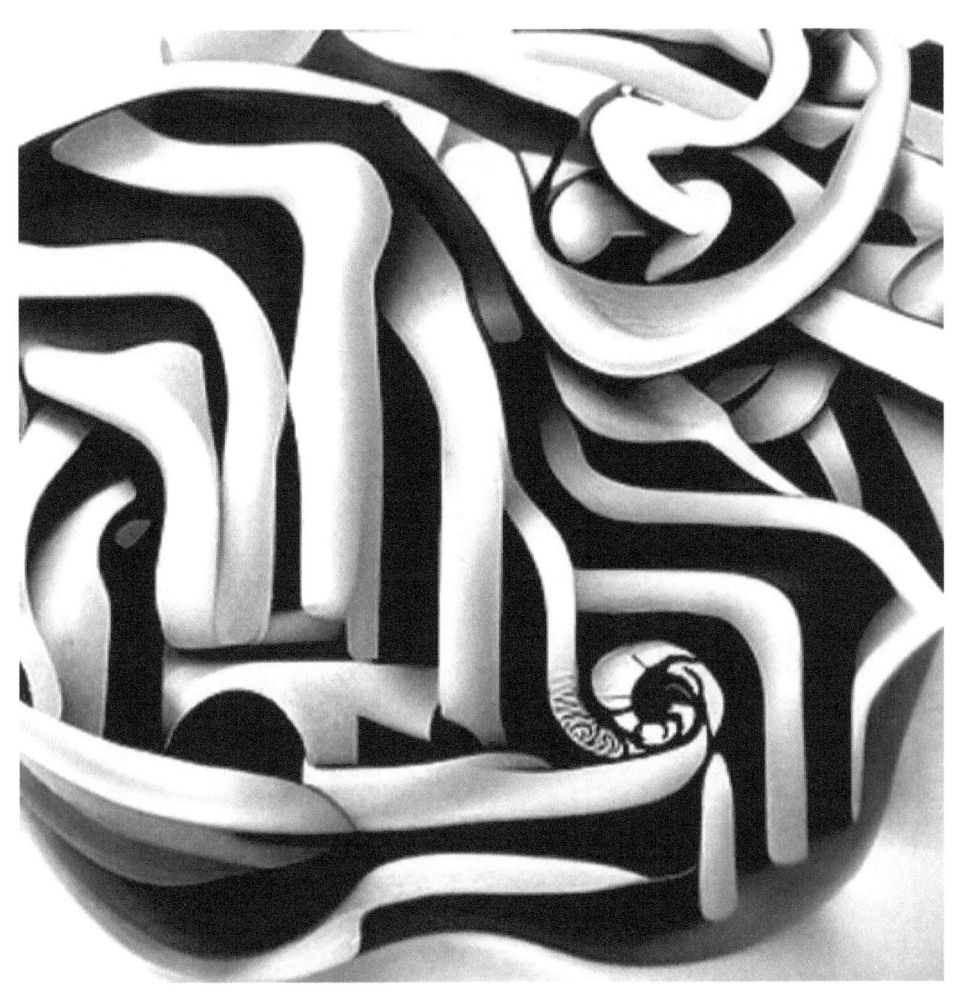

line art, intricate swirly maze, black and white, complex, interesting, futuristic

A.I GENERATION
#17

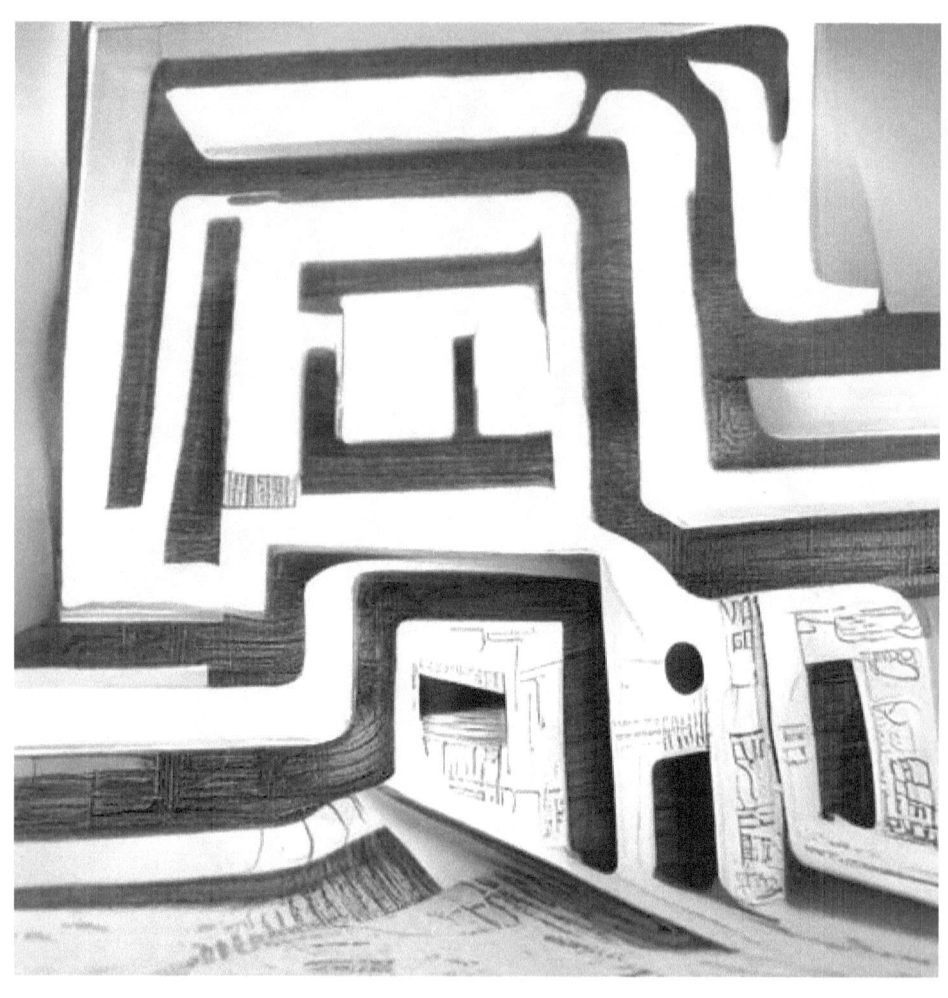

line art, intricate maze, black and white, complex, interesting, futuristic

A.I GENERATION #18

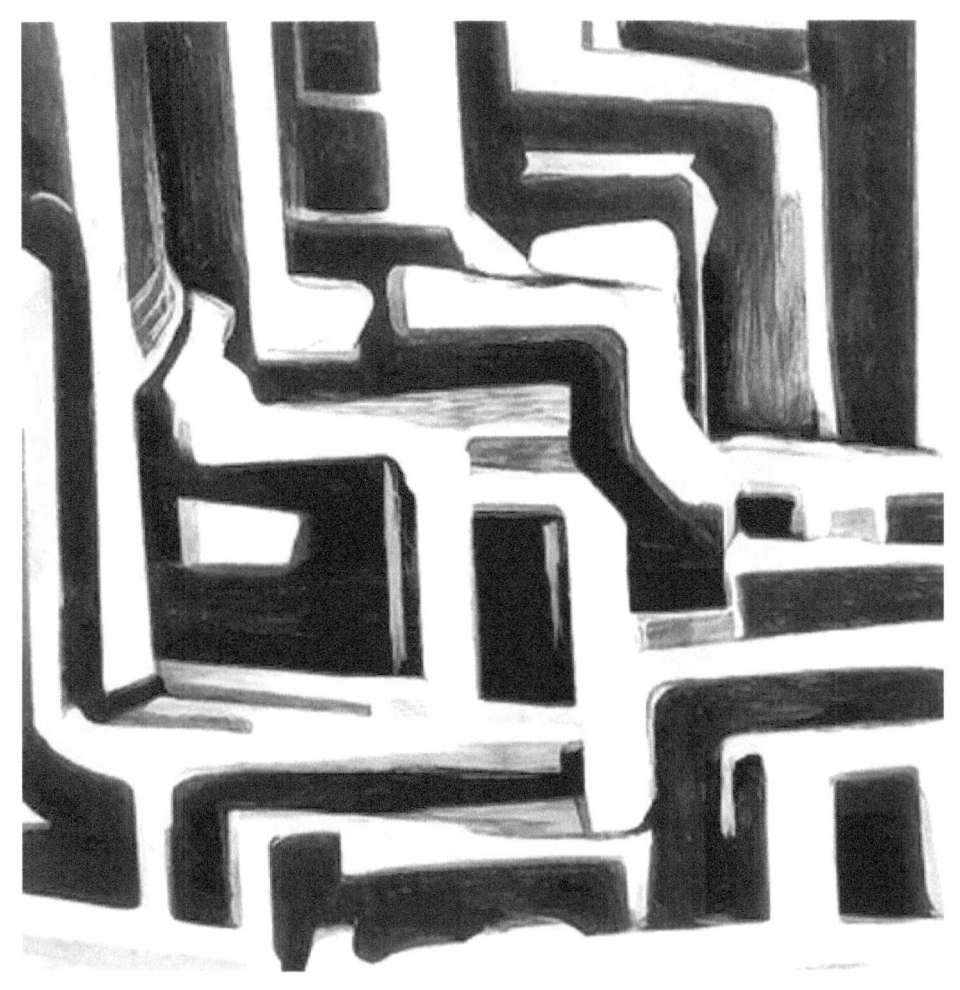

skinny line art, intricate maze, black and white, complex, interesting, futuristic

A.I GENERATION #19

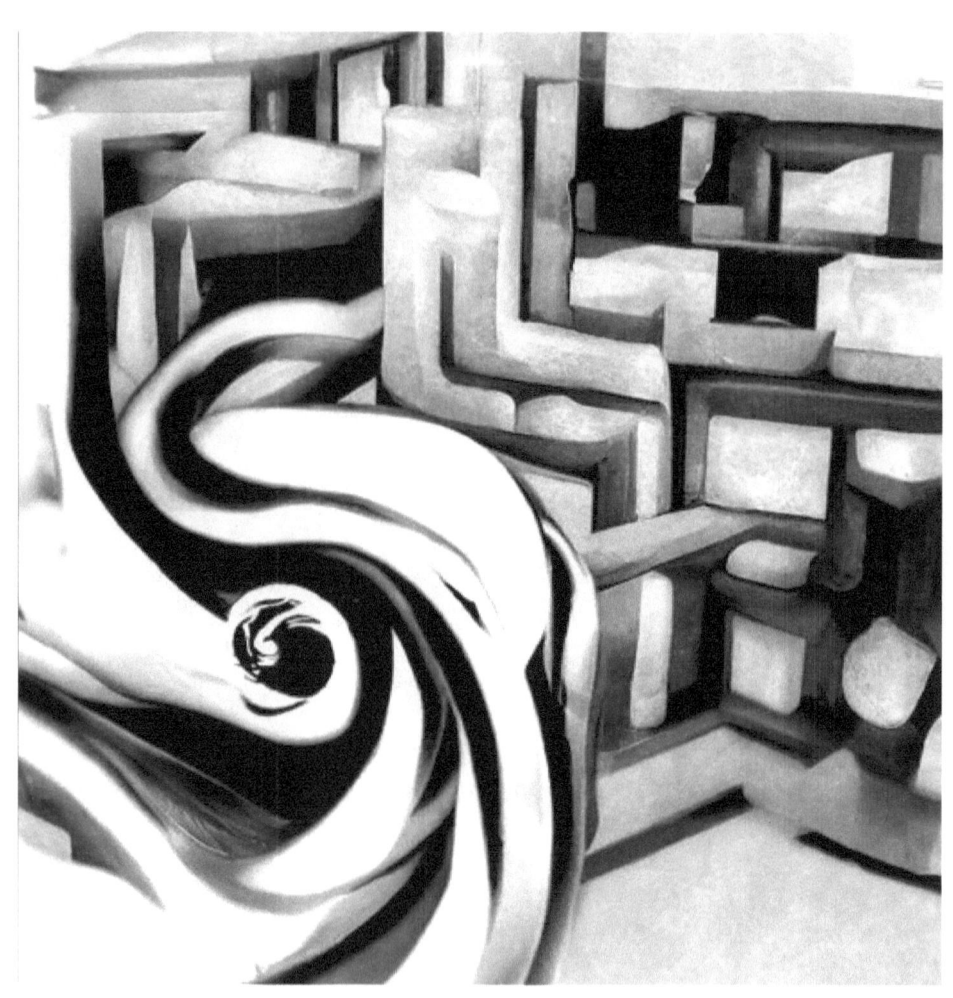

line art, intricate squared swirly maze, black and white, complex, interesting, futuristic, hyper realism, 4k

A.I GENERATION #20

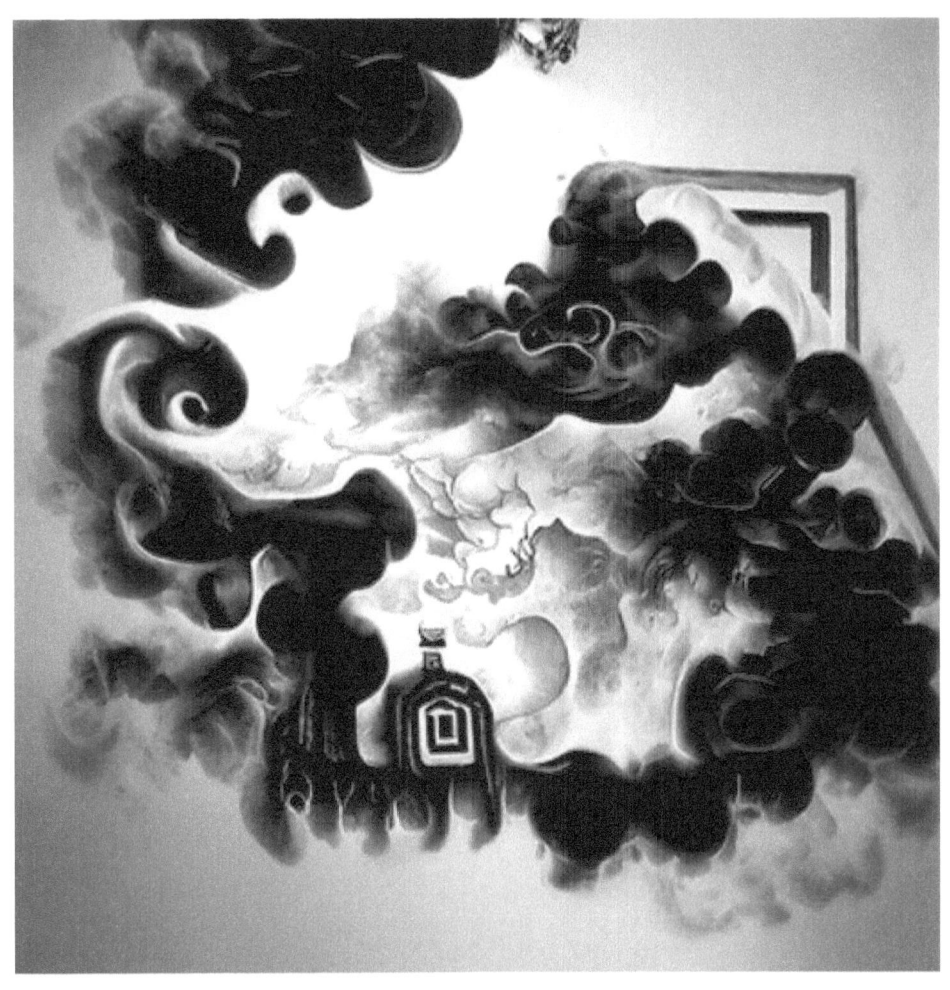

smokey clouds, dark line art, intricate death maze, keyhole, black and white, complex, interesting, realistic

A.I GENERATION
#21

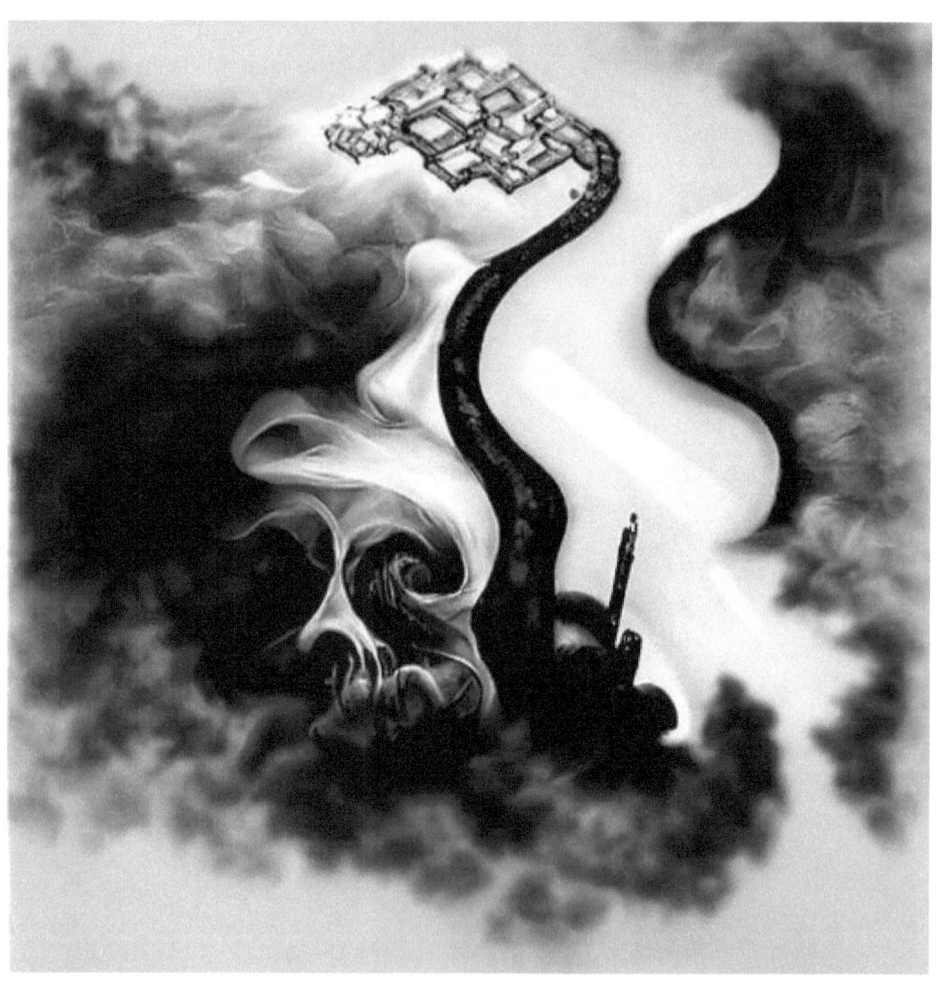

smokey clouds, dark line art, intricate death maze, keyhole, black and white, complex, interesting, realistic

A.I GENERATION
#22

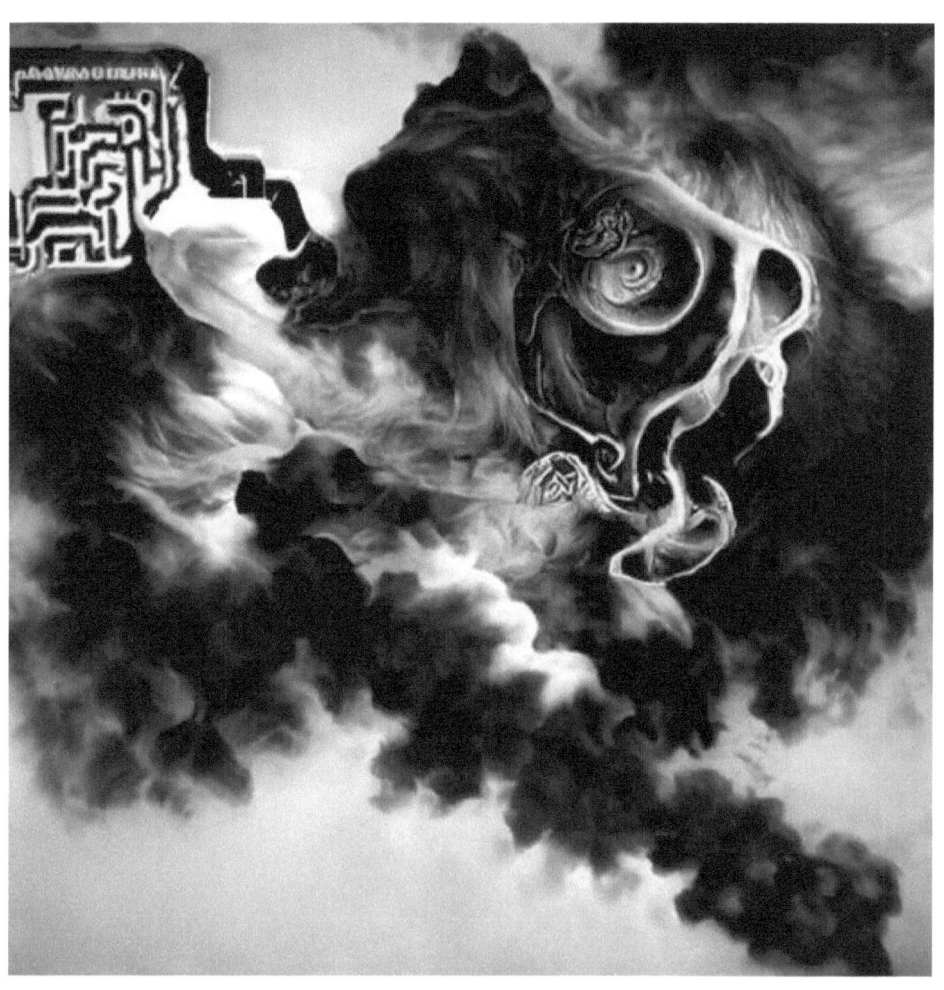

smokey clouds, dark line art, intricate death maze, keyhole, black and white, complex, interesting, realistic

A.I GENERATION
#23

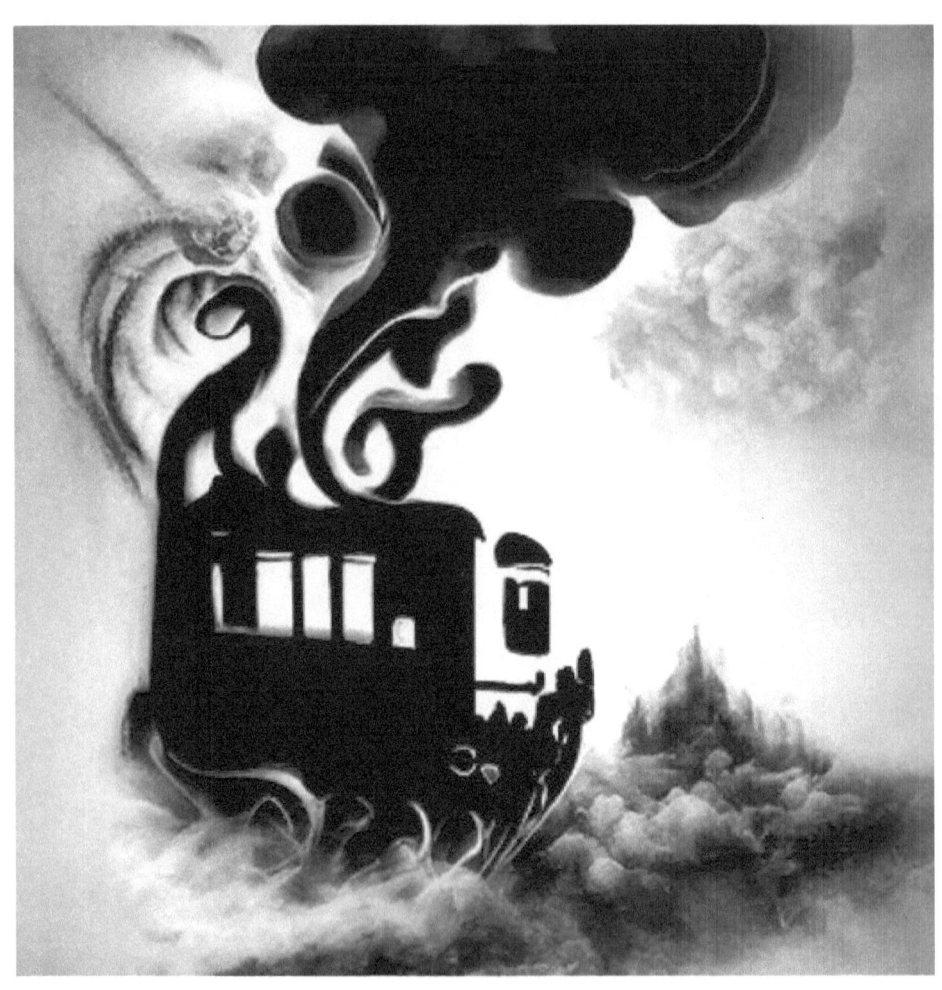

train smokey clouds, dark line art, intricate death maze, keyhole, black and white, complex, interesting, realistic

A.I GENERATION #24

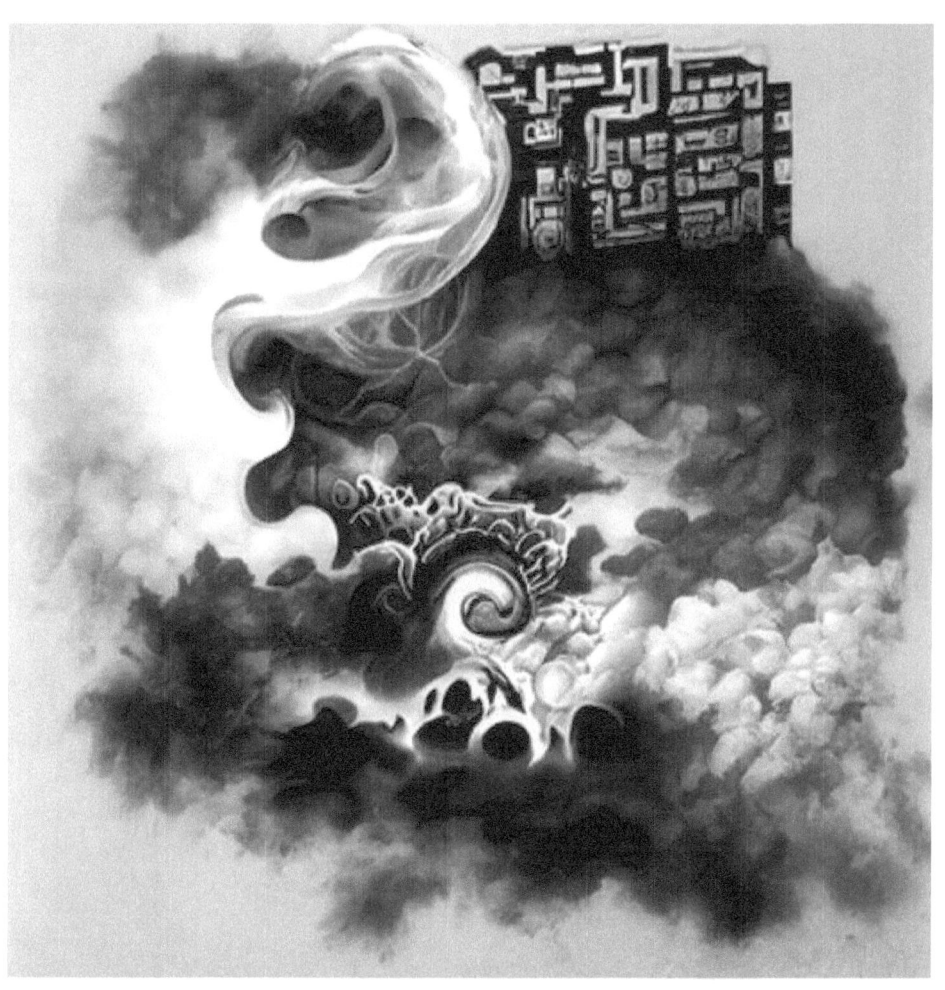

smokey clouds, dark line art, intricate death maze, keyhole, black and white, complex, interesting, realistic

A.I GENERATION
#25

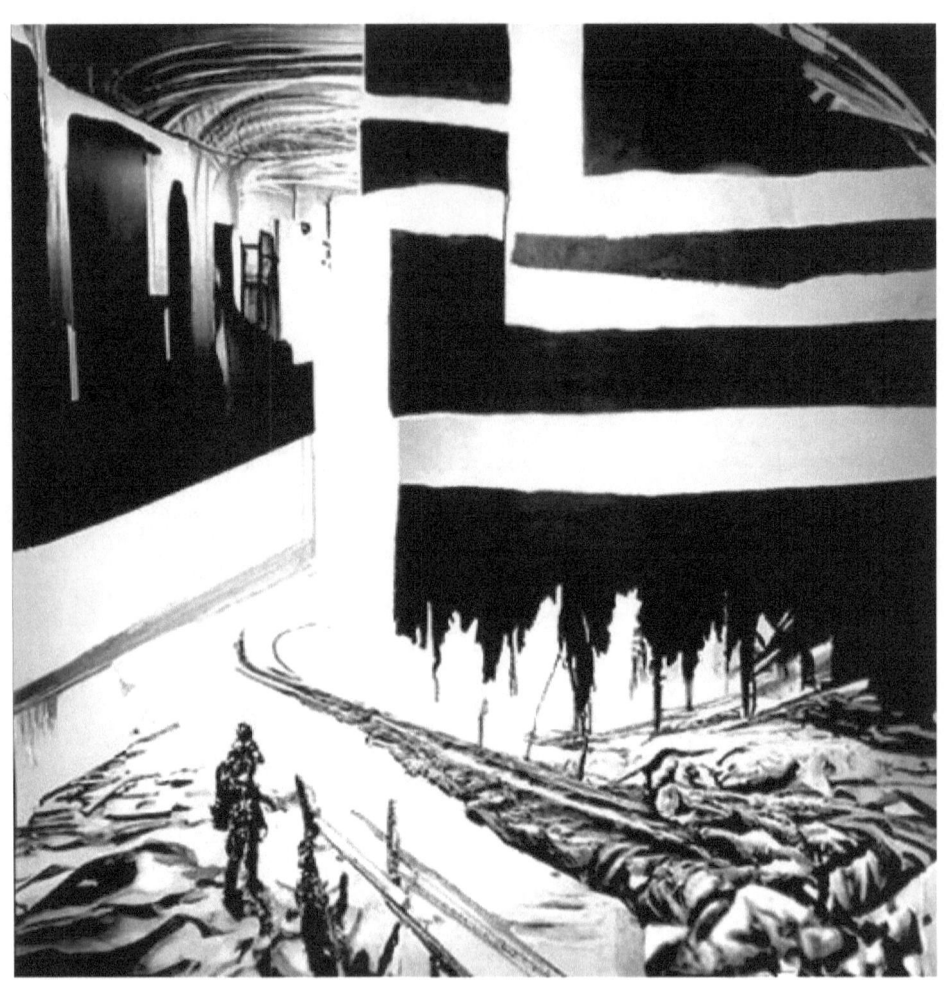

thin dark line art, intricate death maze, black and white, complex, interesting, realistic

A.I GENERATION
#26

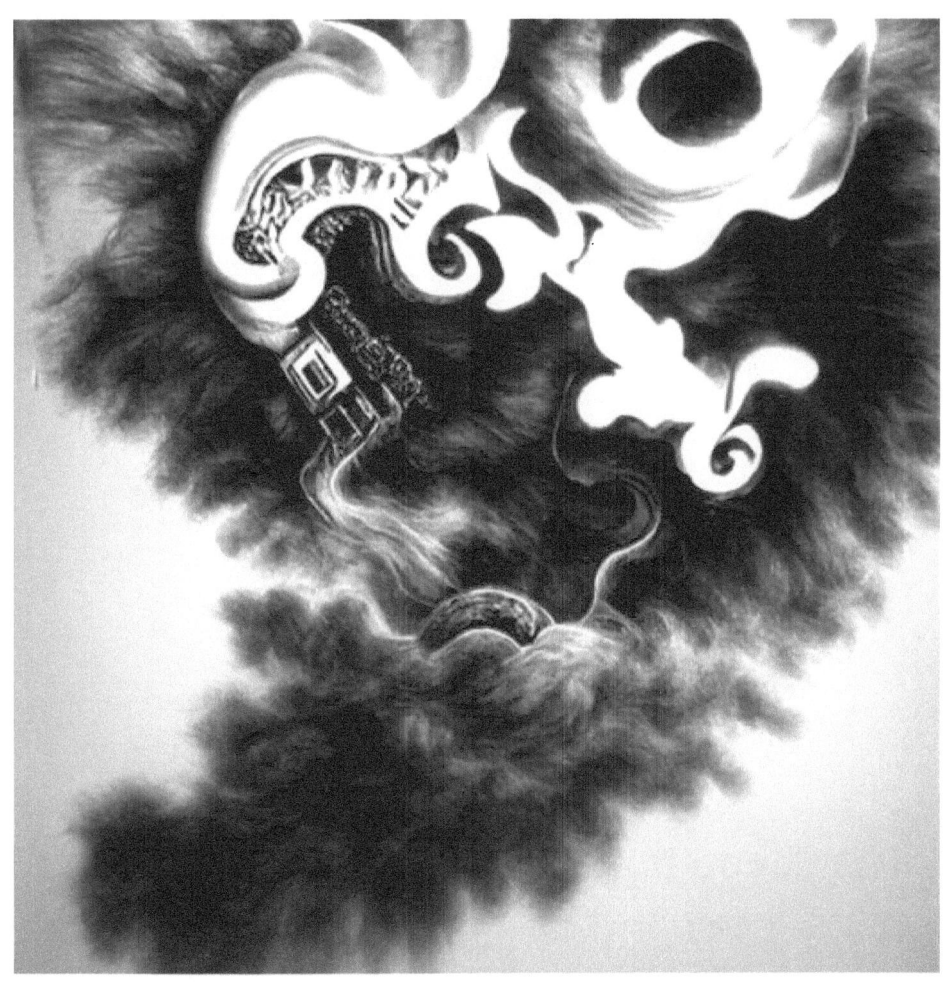

smokey clouds, dark line art, intricate death maze, keyhole, black and white, complex, interesting, realistic

END

Thank you for enjoying the first edition of Inside the mind of A.I, more coming soon...

www.ingramcontent.com/pod-product-compliance
Lightning Source LLC
Chambersburg PA
CBHW031518210526
45464CB00007B/2962